# WHAT MAKES AN INSECT?

## THE ANIMAL KINGDOM

Lynn M. Stone

The Rourke Book Co., Inc.
Vero Beach, Florida 32964

PHOTO CREDITS
All photos © Lynn M. Stone

EDITORIAL SERVICES:
Penworthy Learning Systems

**Library of Congress Cataloging-in-Publication Data**

Stone, Lynn M.
    What Makes an Insect? / by Lynn M. Stone.
        p. cm. — (The Animal Kingdom)
    Includes index
    Summary: Discusses the habits, bodies, and different kinds of
insects and their relationships with people.
    ISBN 1-55916-192-2
    1. Insects—Juvenile literature.  [1. Insects]  I. Title  II. Series:
Stone, Lynn M.    Animal Kingdom.
QL467.2.S79  1997
595.7—dc21                                              96–52190
                                                            CIP
                                                             AC

**Printed in the USA**

# TABLE OF CONTENTS

Insects                        5
Habits of Insects              6
Kinds of Insects               9
Where Insects Live            11
Bodies of Insects             14
Amazing Insects               16
Predator and Prey             19
Baby Insects                  20
People and Insects            22
Glossary                      23
Index                         24

# INSECTS

Little animals that swim, crawl, creep, run, fly, and bite are everywhere. Many of the ones we know best are insects.

Insects are **invertebrate** (in VER tuh BRAYT) animals with six legs. Invertebrates are animals without a backbone or inside skeleton.

Many little animals, of course, have more—or fewer—than six legs. Spiders, for example, have eight legs. They are not insects. Centipedes have dozens of legs and earthworms have none. They are not insects either.

*A black swallowtail butterfly balances on its six legs.*

## HABITS OF INSECTS

Insects move about, eat, rest, search for mates, and sometimes build homes. Most insects lead short lives. A few kinds, or **species** (SPEE sheez), live only for a few days or hours.

Some insects **migrate** (MY grayt). They make long distance journeys, usually in fall and spring.

Insects have no voices, but several make loud noises with their wings or legs. Locusts, crickets, and katydids are nighttime noisemakers.

Some insects spin silk and wrap themselves in a home called a cocoon.

*A cecropia moth spends most of its lifetime in this silky cocoon where it changes from a larva into an adult.*

# KINDS OF INSECTS

The variety of insects is huge. The tiny fruitfly is an insect. So, too, are the big, beautiful, wide-winged moths.

Scientists are still busy finding and naming insects. They locate thousands of new insect species each year. They have already named nearly one million kinds. They will probably find millions more.

Scientists place insects in many different family groups. Moths and butterflies for example, are more alike than different. They belong to the same insect family.

*Walking sticks are related to the praying mantis and other long insects called mantids.*

## WHERE INSECTS LIVE

Insects live almost everywhere, including the edge of icy Antarctica.

Most insects live on land. They are in deserts, forests, grasslands, fields, and caves.

Insects live in the ground. They live under the bark of trees. They live in leaves and in the ears of corn. A few even burrow into people!

A few species live in the oceans. Others live in cold, racing streams and steaming hot pools.

*Plant-eating locust hides from predators by looking like its surroundings on a South Dakota prairie.*

*Insect activity spreads powdery pollen from one plant to another. Pollen helps plants to produce more plants.*

Feelers, like the fan-shaped pair of a polyphemus moth, help insects sense movements and odors around them.

## BODIES OF INSECTS

You can often tell an adult insect by its body. It has three main parts—head, **thorax** (THOR ax), and **abdomen** (AB duh men).

An insect's mouthparts, eyes, and feelers are part of its head. Most insects have two eyes and two feelers.

If an insect has wings, they're attached to the middle part of the body, the thorax. The six legs are also on the thorax.

The abdomen holds eggs, food, and some body organs.

*Dragonfly, warming at dawn, clearly shows the three body sections of a typical insect: head, thorax, and abdomen.*

## AMAZING INSECTS

Some large moths have amazing wingspreads—up to 10 inches (25 centimeters) across. The largest insect body, though, belongs to the four-inch (10 centimeters) Goliath beetle.

Leaf-cutter ants are amazing because they grow their own food! They bring leaf bits to their burrows. The leaves begin to rot. A **fungus** (FUNG gus) grows on the leaves, and the ants eat the fungus.

Some insects look like thorns, leaves, and sticks. Fireflies glow in darkness. The stag beetle has huge jaws that look like deer antlers.

*Bright colors may draw attention, but sharp spines on this moth larva warn predators away.*

# PREDATOR AND PREY

Many insects are **predators** (PRED uh terz). They hunt and kill other insects or small animals for food, or **prey** (PRAY). Dragonflies and assassin bugs are common insect predators in North America.

Insects are important prey for many kinds of spiders, frogs, lizards, snakes, fish, birds, and mammals.

Most insect species are plant-eaters. They eat fruit, grass, leaves, and even wood. Mosquitoes feed on blood. A few insect species eat clothing.

*A predator robber fly hugs its prey, a sulphur butterfly.*

## BABY INSECTS

Many young insects do not have six legs. That is because most insects grow up by going through four steps, or stages. One stage doesn't look much like the others.

The first stage is the egg. the second stage is the **larva** (LAHR vuh). Insect larvas are often wormlike caterpillars.

The third stage is the **pupa** (PU puh). During that stage, the larva changes into an adult. A moth pupa hides in a cocoon.

If an insect survives the early stages, it becomes an adult.

*Cecropia moth lays eggs through a tube in her abdomen.*

## PEOPLE AND INSECTS

Everyone deals with insects. They are part of our lives almost everywhere we go. We slap some, trap some, and admire others.

Some insects are dangerous. They bite, sting, or carry diseases.

Others are just pests. They nibble our gardens or woodwork. They make loud noises at night.

Many insects, however, are beautiful, and many, many more are very important. Insect activity helps plants make more plants. No group of animals is more important to the balance of nature.

# Glossary

**abdomen** (AB duh men) — the third main body part of insects and one which contains important organs

**fungus** (FUNG gus) — any one of a large family of plantlike growths

**invertebrate** (in VER tuh BRAYT) — an animal without a backbone; insects, for example

**larva** (LAHR vuh) — an early stage of life in insects and certain other animals

**migrate** (MY grayt) — to travel to a distant place at the same time each year

**predator** (PRED uh ter) — an animal that hunts other animals for food

**prey** (PRAY) — an animal that is hunted by another animal for food

**pupa** (PU puh)— the third stage of life of most insects; the stage between being a larva and an adult

**species** (SPEE sheez) — within a group of closely related animals, one certain kind, such as a *monarch* butterfly

**thorax** (THOR ax) — the second major body section of an insect; the section with wings and legs

# INDEX

abdomen   14
ants, leaf-cutter   16
assassin bugs   19
beetle   16
   Goliath   16
   stag   16
butterflies   9
caterpillars   20
centipedes   5
cocoon   6, 20
dragonflies   19
eggs   14, 20
eyes   14
feelers   14
fireflies   16
head   14

insects   5, 6, 9, 11, 14,
   16, 20, 22
   species of   6
larva   20
legs   5, 14, 20
mosquitoes   19
moths   9, 16
mouthparts   14
plants   19, 22
predators   19
prey   19
pupa   20
spiders   5, 19
thorax   14
wings   14